Copyright @ 2021

All rights reserved. No part of this publication may be reproduced, distributed, or transmitted in any form.

Thank You!

We create our books with love and great care.

Your opinion will help us to improve this book and create new ones.

We love to hear from you.

Please, support us and leave a review!

www.ingramcontent.com/pod-product-compliance
Lightning Source LLC
LaVergne TN
LVHW060158080526
838202LV00052B/4168